What's mine is ours

NISH VERMA

What's mine is ours

NISH VERMA

PAPER TOWNS
PUBLISHERS

First published by
Papertowns Publishers
72, Vishwanath Dham Colony,
Niwaru Road, Jhotwara,
Jaipur, 302012

What's Mine is Ours

ISBN Print Book – 978-93-94670-19-8

Cover by Neha Agrawal
nehaa.2089@gmail.com

Acknowledgement:

I would like to thank my mom and dad. Also, the publisher of this book.

Index:

Lily of the flower........1
Empty your mind........2
A familiar setting........3
Neatly Impressed........4
Is this called realizing?........5
Dare me........6
Just quarrels........7
Positive body........8
Where to bury some truth?........9
Assumption........10
Again........11
A Past question is a past........12
A bad day I made myself........13
This city........15
Words in a Puzzle........16
A place beyond the hills........17
Got a bone to pick........19
Fun?........20
Alarm clock........21
Art of dying is beautiful........22
Fuckboys........23
Fell from the sky........25

I see too much....26
He....28
A new friend joins the party....30
Pissed off and you'll get it....31
Self summarized....32
To be or not to be....34
Abyss....36
Crash and burn....37
December....38
Seen? good....39
All part of the plan, I just made up....43
Should I say more or less to be real?....44
Moonshine....45
Ofcourse, reality....46
A legend of the Castle Capricorn....47
Atleast intuitive....49
Won't I?....51
This spirit....52
Queen of a butter paper....54
Cut you like cold wood....57
I cling onto....58
Fixed with both sides....59
Strings....60
No one without no other....61

Hypocrisy....63
Can't go on without you....64
True story....66
Die young and leave a pure looking corpse....67
Do you really understand me?....68
Oii ego, what you writing?....69
Petty little me....71
Girl with raven colored hair....72
A peaceful imagination....73
Phoenix....74
Angry, get over it....76
You don't know....78
Just eight and eight stuff....79
Cut the chase, back to my place....80
Into a rage, I fly....81

Lily of the flower

In the season of lily of the flower,
The lily of the flower expected love...
All the skies till the horizon frowned upon the dear,
But never could give up,
As a lot of courage is needed...to live here and with this,
Till eternity.
With a gentle smile she would fall home
At the end of dusk.
And eyes would glitter with a new dawn.
But the time was cruel...
Not for this day but until the sun was sacrificed..
For her choice in,
Living with vanity.

Empty your mind

It's not a disgrace or bad fate,
That a world full of empathetics
But nothingness for each else.
Always has a good start,
But we take a turmoil and change,
Something you need to keep fixed.
So, you walk around with your empty heart
And a body of lies wanting a nobody,
Drinking water from the lakes which were just meant to dry out,
Eventually.
To help you see,
See that you belong in an ocean,
This vast and never-ending cycle...
Where love will always be there and nothing can probe or take it.
You give and give but it's never-ending,
And boundaries were just in our mind.

A familiar setting

Well, well and a well.
Here is this, yet again.
Snacks with bread,
Laying out your rest.
Do I mean something?
Of course.
Every day I may confess.
On four or three,
Strikes like something slick.
Turning sober into sobriety,
Isn't much concerned with this.
Okay, so sounds here big,
Doesn't really mean much every time.
And oh,
Here I am...in this place,
Where someone ran,
But here I come,
Everyday a little less.
Guess, I ran hard but not enough.
But here I come,
And I didn't wish it's a way...
Take it as you may.

Neatly Impressed

Crashed onto your couch,
Believing in a lethal weapon called love,
Give or take.
Nothing much left to wonder
As a wonderful night was gazing.
All her night stars for us.
And your dog which I thought was a cat,
With his little paws and beautiful eyes,
Ran to the kitchen,
Falling in the smell of soup.
He thought it was for him....
No boy, it's for me.
I elected my thoughts in my mind
To impress you with which ones...
They all were blossoms
But I think I'm a democrat,
Even when you fell for my regal aura...
It's okay, love. I'll buy you the moon,
We will kill the rules...
Causing havoc on streets and
Building pools of blood
And pool tables, too...
Whatever you want, babe.

Is this called realizing?

So, I was wearing black shoes
On a winter night,
For a west side where snow never dries.
And I could be friends with wolves,
Rule them and care for, of course.
But in this constant movement of vehicles
I drifted upon to something bigger
And, as usual, the negative came first,
To draw my attention more deeply
And thoroughly for it....
In with some consistency, I went
To conjure a thought for a conversation
I had where I was where converse shoes left
And he figured me out...you know,
Just like that...
Said, my mind and body are a conjunction,
You can't consider the wrong concerns.

Dare me

Dare me to move,
Dare me to do things that I don't want to.
Throw these lies and throw it some more.
I am still getting up...

Sun is fine but it seems it isn't...
Carrying it round and round.
Then down, down, down
But I am still getting up.

You see, all I sought and she...
Was time with each other.
Now you go, bury it far.
At a place where they think I can't reach,
Even with a million seconds to spare or waste.
And I will still get up.

Just quarrels

Don't make me wait,
I worked hard for this day..
I waited and I waited patiently...
For you,
For this moment.
You wanna make this right?
And then you said it could be too late.
Let it burn away,
Burn my heart with it.
I think too much,
Said so less.
But you know it, what everyone tries to know...
And I know it, what everyone tries to know.

I would take this night,
Into all the nights of my life,
For the rest of my life..
Cause only now is all I've ever been alive..

Positive body

On the brighter side of life,
I could run on mountains..
Like its presence wasn't even a problem.
On the brighter side of life,
I cut air, put it in my cup
And drink it like tea.
On the brighter side of life,
I get no red lights
Or the sound of arrogance through their horns, in my ears.
On the brighter side of life,
I laugh a lot,
It's us with a better point of view.
On the brighter side,
I chill about everything.
Leaving on this side for today.

Where to bury some truth?

I used to visit a friend.
A couple lived next door...
He was calm, chilled out, you know;
She was a hot head, but kind.
They were great,
They were around my age.
From my point of view,
Didn't really have much, didn't really need much.
Married, great.
She was due for a baby in november,
Not really planned much on anything.
Life gave this and some problems called that.
Around them some said,
'What a bummer this will be'.
Not gonna give a fuck about what anyone says....can hear the walls say.
'No, this is the best...you two go good. You need to work more and you need to smoke less; everything else is just alright already', I said.
Whenever I go there, I just say that.
But somewhere deep down, I envy them.
My heart says this was all we really wanted....
True love and ignorance.

Assumption

When I saw some sweet dreams,
Falling in all the right sides,
I never lied....
When I hear some of your life,
I have to end my word.
I never sigh.
All seem so pale in the moonlight,
Cause I never know,
How to deal when it's all bright...
That's my style.
Four times I added three to one,
I never lost my intentions.
In the middle of this year,
We told so much,
When there was nothing left to wonder.

Again

Again,
Here's my home,
I try not to run anymore.
Come again?
Sorry, I often don't go in these conversations anymore.
Rather wonder in a land of fairy and values.
I tried to go in my direction,
Made myself believe that I'd be good,
On this very day.
Trained some senses to be sensible
And more or less practical,
But I made none...
And none comes into this pot,
Where I've been throwing different shells of myself,
Ever since I was twelve.
To be made and believed again....
In that someday,
Where I'll be understood, or less just by myself.

A Past question is a past

Summer wind around a haze,
Far from the horns of some chaotic place.
It is better or at least some days...
Clinging onto life,
Even though it's so....hmm, forget it.
I fucking love it.
They all seem so happy and nice,
No disorder and a need for any realized restrictions.
Like the first love you experience,
Everything's just in a perfect space.

Now the night comes,
And I go to my hotel room,
With these bottles of wine
And bottles of happy faced friends....
With this chick whose been eyeing me,
Since the morning; ten am.

Is this what you call being a happy person?
Everything about it is materialism.
Anyways, today I realized...
Yes, there's a difference,
Being in love and getting attached are different.
What's it worth, talking about us now, huh?

A bad day I made myself

I woke up feeling good.
A drive one way took an hour and a half,
Normally it takes just thirty-five minutes.

I tried to draw today, but all the shades were bad.
Either too dark where light was necessary,
Or the opposite.

A guy's birthday at work,
Ordered food for everyone; Chicken and rice and
burgers for snacks.
I got none, being a vegetarian,
Everybody ate.

I was wearing my favorite sunglasses...
Today, they broke.
Maybe because sometimes I fall asleep in their eyes.

I tried singing today,
But my voice doesn't sound nice.
Notes were off, no timing...I was off
Usually I'm not that bad, but today...

You fought with your mother,
First thing in the morning.
She cried.
What did you expect?
Presidential elections?
Very good.

This city

This city wants a metamorphosis between wanna be
wild and feeling forgotten.
Sun so bright that the skin needs cosmetics for
resemblance.
This city couldn't be kept calm but still is sleeping.
Water what's left is drained,
There was never no triumph.
This city runs on oils and no one knows where to get
them.
Coming up with schemes and plans,
Aren't needed and are bearing.
This city had squirrels and pigeons which would
shine,
Around grass and trees...way too many.
Now we rust on clothes and machines.
This city has a lost culture,
Whatever was left of it,
To people who will judge you on their mother tongue.
But we like it, don't we?
I'm doing it right now, too, you can read,
I feel bad and I feel bad too often.

Clearly; The city is not a concrete jungle,
It's a human zoo.

Words in a Puzzle

Burn ego,
No one won,
No one will.
Think, you do already.
  Where?
  Fight.
  Fight yourself,
  Fight them and everyone.
It's not that, you know.
Find, keep it for days and weeks.
Search?
Won't get anything.
No one knows where to go, where will be.
Sleep, empty heart...yours,
  Everyday.
  Give hope and assurance...Mayday.
  Lie and lie and lie more,
  Do good.
Maybe around,
Empty cars and empty faces.
Crawling above things only been respected.
Be what's left,
Whatever's left.
Worth the trouble?

A place beyond the hills

There's a place,
Way from this current.
Won't bother whether it's up or down.
Only knows and goes alone.

You cross all the walls,
Cross all the spring trees
And roses become just your imagination.
There isn't any nature or feeling of it.
For clawed predators,
Fight each other to gain their opinion.
On you, over you.
It doesn't matter...

Run into the deep until it becomes black.
So, you'll feel cold and then learn to keep it.
Never gonna melt now.
Towards a door, you thought would be bright
Or may lead you back.
It doesn't.
So, you sit there,

Where time stops and you too won't care for the clocks.
Skin burns and head hurts,
Can't remember hunger.
Sit there,
And stare with eyes closed.
It doesn't matter.

Some days you'll probably sleep on it,
Some days you won't.
Some days you wish you could.
But you'll learn something new and true.
Worth the effort or not?
Maybe it is or maybe it's not.
Some people say it wasn't there,
Wasn't there, illogical and fake.
Some people don't need it.
A lot of them barely felt it.
Few know about but don't want,
They run...into entertain, escape and everything.
Few feel it every day,
They accept.
Is it a gift?

Got a bone to pick

Hey, look around...
One sheep,
Two sheep,
There, a sheep,
Another sheep.
Look, sheep,
Run, sheep,
Talk, sheep,
Sheep, sheep,
Sleep sheep.
Fucking sheep..
With a minus thought for every solution,
But you got that.

Fun?

Why is it so hard to have fun?
My friends are kind,
Have a good heart,
Young.
Why is it so hard to have fun?
Always worried
And a lot of struggle for every once,
Desire.
Saturn says you know the reasons,
It's not the right time,
Work the bullshit up,
Everything will come.
Yeah, okay. Why is it so hard to have fun?
Isn't too much to ask,
Everyone has some.
At least I don't hold hands to pass time,
Or just for lust.
Don't get me started on that.
Shouldn't be so hard for us,
If I had to run three sixty kilometers every month...
Just to see the one I love.
Oops...out of context,
All of a sudden.

Alarm clock

Consumed in,
Long blankets on my warm body
And it rains....
This rain doesn't affect me,
It just soaks in my mud.
Place to be at eight,
Must leave a reminder.

Art of dying is beautiful

Today isn't a new day.
Far from shores and far from rays.
Just me and my friend, brain.
Like I am and maybe it's me.
Just doesn't learn,
Never wanna feel.

Today isn't a new day.
Don't tell me that I can't see.
When winds line up for me,
I'll deny it,
Won't accept it,
Not gonna fall for them.
As I still hold on yesterdays...
Till death parts me.

Self-destruction.
It's an art.
You'll know, no one can destroy you like yourself.
Not a lot of people are good at it either,
Like I expected.

Fuckboys

No, you don't treat her right...
You don’t fuck her right.
Everything you talk is a lie.
And she won't remember you either,
Like your mother doesn't remember you.
Bye.

Passion for few days
Or passionate every minute.
Is it about paying your debt?
About living every day as new,
Forgetting what you had yesterday.
Moving on?
A desire which doesn't belong.
A rainbow for eye or darkness even with sight.
Selfish?
I can be selfish?
Each their own we playing?
A nice word, I should say.
Think that everyone's brain in controlled
By ten-year olds from a superior dimension,
On a laptop playing us as a fun game.
Now, that's a good use of imagination.
Well, my player is high...
Should have seen a manual before entering this time.

Fell from the sky

For once, not on the blind side.
Version not gonna stick in mind.
Its fever...dry and bites.
Night is never easy.

For once, call it a truce.
Might offer less than nothing at all.
With words tend to be hurtful every day,
In ways that can't be shared.
As the water hits the ground
But never breaks.

Introspection of self-image,
Oh! What a shame.
What do you think?
It all stays the same.
A denial accompanying different shades,
And then I love falling in my desires,
Makes me feel like I fell from the sky.
Burning the rush in my riots,
Makes me feel like I fell from the sky.

I see too much

Hey there?
Sometimes I see you looking very pale.
Did you see me feeding all my wrath to dust?
Probably not that bright, quietly messed up.
Last night you ditched out,
Puked it up,
All the bullshit thoughts....
There... you seemed fucked up, too.
Went on and used the tools,
But still nights are a little easier for you.
Gotta learn this word 'Hello'.
Seems like loneliness is all we ever do.
Now we go out and the prediction causes trouble.
Cared.
Saved the pain for daylight,
It will be easier for me and you.

At the time of some thought,
Blinked for guidance,
As I just can't give up.
Though, I tried a lot.
He doesn't listen to me.
In some shores saw a way,
They said,
Of fulfillment but still uncertain.
I didn't believe it.
Not much to offer on those.
Partially signed some resistance.
It was just so hard for me to carry on.
Though, I tried a lot.
He just doesn't listen to me
Outskirts of a perfect boredom,
Heard poetry isn't any justification.
Just writing....it's easy,
Anyone can do it.
Yes, only with a mind of your own.
And then make it sound like you don't crumble,
By taking off subjects.
Faking...
As common as bad air now.

He

He, you asked?
In some ways,
On some days,
For some moods, as she fell for,
Some other.
Cause some sense I guess,
Like I want some symmetry
Or order in my distorted life...
Or you could say,
An identity crisis, every other step.
Like you follow a retard line
From my mind and it doesn't matter.
I'll make ice cubes out of my eyeballs,
If I ever fell into this,
Admiration based on pretentiousness.
My heart won't accept,
My heart says something else.
So, blame it on my bet or something irrelevant.
Between this perfect questioning
And constant interrogation,
It led to this.
Gonna leave this behind....
But I know I will,

Run back to get back.
As nothing makes sense
And nothing ever will.

A new friend joins the party

Another guess.
Trees seem to be blunt today.
As I approached one,
This brown dusted lake of leaves.
This is an imagination,
Justification comes only in stupid games.
Or to say that I am filled with unavailability,
In a constant state of time,
To be made to believe by this life,
For the rest of my life.
I don't hate it,
Always willing to throw this...
Day of any week or minute which ends in seconds.
Like it doesn't matter.
In this rush, where I only attract a stand for misdirection.
Once I invited chaos to dinner....
We shared the same meal together.
He said he will take care of me
And I'm never leaving him.

Pissed off and you'll get it

Remember, back in the old times,
After wars or at carnivals
When all the men used to gather,
Sit around and drink and act funny.
With their beer bellies and forgettable faces,
Pretending cool.
And then these women would come around
And dance, to entertain the stupid who liked that.
With their beautiful bodies and dull minds,
Getting used by the junk males of society.

Do you wanna know where it is today?
At least women got paid for such jobs earlier...
And the guys were, you know, men.
Where is it?

Self summarized

In a way, I brought some decency
From times and times ago.
Does this free my illusions?
Or am I still possessed in them.

Kind of a scared thought,
I don't like to roam around it a lot.
Like to build it up to some extend
And then let loose for most of my day.
Now I seem to understand,
As I was just trying to sell my revenge.
In time I will make peace with the past,
For it never existed except in my heart.

A way to go, In the end,
I end up back to the start.
That's fine as long as I don't become corrupted...
Like most fuckers are.
There, my ego.

Nature of things...when I came to see my reality,
I often avoid it.
Only made me crumble to pieces,

Every time I sensed the arrow...
Coming to rip my heart again.
There, my protective nature...
Left by myself amidst the darkness
Where I can't see the dawn.
I go through the same over and over again,
And then I write about it over and over....
With an imagination in a concrete loop.
And hey, you are somehow the same, too...
So, time for consideration for you.
There, my narcissistic approach...
And then to avoid conversations,
Play make believe with dolls and cars.

To be or not to be

I sat on this bench,
To be aware of the front.
Saw some silence to which I developed,
An awe to whom and what.
And then I started considering this and
I thought I should think that, too.
It followed like a razor blade intense energy
Of which I have no control over, yet.
So, you see where I sit?

But anyways,
There is her and a bundle of him...
I wonder about the middle ground
But my mind can now see the real ground.
To be or not to be, I suggested myself.
Where they pulled her fifteen thousand buck
clothing...
Slowly, and she didn't even know it.
Every other day, an inch by inch.
And went in to stood in line with their masked
perfections
To give her a sense of protection.
They said with confidence, but no.

They don't.

They really don't.

To be or not to be, I lost.

Abyss

Well, I've been feeling like a bird in a cage.
Swallowed and narrowed down because of some frail.
Is it my own fault?
That I can dream...
Because all I can imagine are places,
Bright and way far in the distance.
For my head to even wonder such things
Or to find happiness through it.
Oh! What a shame.
To nights where it goes all in an abyss,
Indecisiveness is my prime minister...
Which led me to this depth.
Where I've been burdened for some cause
Or some reason to live in or believe in
Which I never wanted or chose.

Crash and burn

Crash and burn,
I remember it being fun.
For some while the wildlife shows would help.
As you predicted, I looked everywhere.
All the wolves and concrete...
All the people with discipline,
And everything which plays set.
Fun.

Crash and burn.
Long faced skies
And I'll never understand their whys.
Probably a nail in my head,
By the creator.
Delayed, and I play predictions with delays now...
They said time is precious...
Is it?

Crash and burn.
Drawn towards whiskey doors.
Out of evenings for my beloved, you.
And then I said I'll make it in time,
I've got this picture of us kids in my mind.
Pathetic.
Not me, you.

December

Every year as December passes me by.
A part of me goes away.
When I was young, I frowned up on this desolation.
As today was all of me
Made me feel as myself complete.

A nothin I could do...
And I realized it as I grew,
As push came to shove.
I just watched myself burn to ashes
And there isn't much crying left, you know.

Every year as December passes me by,
A part of me goes away.
Seclusion and isolation hold my hand with a firm grip.
To take me home and be lost in my ego.
To arrange the held,
Which was always frozen by snow.

Seen? good

I got pretty like a girl.
Then I got wise, voice and chill.
See both sides like a devil,
Sea on both sides for thrill.

Women love cool pool boys.
They didn't like my underworld.
Hide my tattoos, an issue boy....
Police thinking I'm ugly underground.

Twelve to two my pillow talks.
Hey, you lookin at me? Won't you talk?
Don't you see I am the give man..
Don't you see I am the I am.

I fell into a drunk can,
To kitties cuttin my number.
Always taking the first blood.
Many went ocean marathons.

Just a bunch of people dissing...
Twenty percent of my ideas are playing punk,
He's a click not a cult,

Buttercup went run,
Agony.

Double edged, my life.
I don't like fighting but I'm fighting.
Imagine this air making my mom sick...
Planes in the sky but a never-ending conflict.

I see both sides like a devil,
Sea on both sides for thrill.
But it's really just you on my mind.
It's just you and our time.

Free smoke rings in hell,
Snakes don't grind in wells.
Mystic ground hanging off my belt...
But it's all an old style, no chanel.

And then I acted shy, To hold myself up..
But they tied my knees ..
And then gifted...
Something called basketball card plus.

Now I've got your money and it's all cash..
I've got new plans and none are thrash

A rubber band bunch of thousand bucks of gift cards,
My baby got.
Her days end in la la la.
I mean, it's her got.

Form of a beautiful life I envisioned.
You know, perfect days and perfect nights.
Well, there's dust on it now.
An empty lake filled with caterpillars...
I don't like to think,
They belong here.
Have to indulge in various...
To make myself around...
A wrong way to hold on to my belongings.
There aren't left many.
Another spelling error.
Yes, there's an error...
That's why the world turned like this
Or at least from my eyes it did.
Pity for you and pity on me
And I still feel it's more to this than this.
Secretive in nature,
Secretive in words and actions.
Yes, there is more to it than you think there is.

All part of the plan, I just made up

This june could last for four years,
A couple of months and eight wednesdays..
If I don't watch my back
Or clear my head to start things fresh, they said.

No,
It's not my nature..
I dwell on the past...
I would like to continue to smoke the same brand.
It's not part of my plan.
Fixed ideas and fixed bodies, I only asked...
Change is a heartbreak.
I don't like to crumble all the time,
Just to leave patches on places and people..
Whom I am shadowed for.
It's not fair.
It's not gonna be the plan.
Imagination is a bro but you take it back...
Give it to the dumbledore living next door...
Out of my way.

Should I say more or less to be real?

Together we laughed,
When the sky sent flowers for us.
And when we fought,
Only then the sun was a burn.
Together in a distance,
We held expectations.
The more I learned, the less I deal...
Should I say more or less to be real?

Moonshine

For I've come so far, my dear...
Collecting shattered fears.
Lost in my illusions,
I think I need them.

Every moment I spared...
My dear, came so late...
I almost didn't care.

Don't strangle yourself,
Into the unknown..
For you may wish,
You were never there.
In between places like those....
I made a home.

Walk around troubled in the night life...
I walked around bitter in the night sky...
Walk around troubled in the night sky.
Until the moonshine.

Ofcourse, reality

It's been raining for three evenings now.
The thunder god is pleased with my actions.
He grants his approval.

A minute more I spend
And a minute less I cared for.
This loop...I can't seem to figure out.
I am almost on my knees here...
Taking refuge in cheaters and disgraced.
Is it meant to help me out?
I don't have any design or a need of circumstance,
To impress you.
With my love in her closed eyes,
Wandered with hopelessness....
Or am I the hopeless one all along?

A legend of the Castle Capricorn

Me, alone...My goal - nothing.
You, enough...run away
Else I will show you your truth.

Sun is burning on my skin,
Sun will see me taking it in...
Sun will see me eating him.

I know your bullshit.
I rose from it after all and you made it your home.
No fear can cut my courage.
No one stands my way.
Justice is what I follow,
Fair is who I am...
No more answers about me to you, run.

I loved, I cared...our bed.
See now,
You rot with them.
You are getting fucked by dogs.
You deserve it.
That's your punishment,
That's your karma.

Someone will always be fair,
To me and to everyone,
Everyone on this plain.

Money is getting rolled by my little finger.
Royalty is what I eat...
Royalty is now what I sweat.
Looking for good but always watching the bad.
In control even in fire or a tsunami.
A loner but not lonely.
Anything I desire becomes mine.
Know how to do it,
My duty.

This won't work this time.
A burden now.
Need to eat ice cream and watch sitcoms.
Some will need it,
Some will keep it.

Atleast intuitive

Trouble on the door, said..
Your life revolves around love.
Enough food, babe, but here you starve.
I said I like simple things but I like it hard.
A shadow whispered in my ear..
She'll be your past.
Oh! No.

Well, I cried all day wearing back sided shoes....
I made a simple verse chorus song to impress you.
They said, It's dull and nothing much....
A shadow came by,
She'll be my past.
Oh! No.

All dream,
while asleep in the night.
But,
Some dream,
With their eyes wide open.
All the time.
Those are the most dangerous people in the world,
Watch out.

Won’t I?

So you said that,
You'll wait there,
Where the sky is always pretty
And we won't end here.

Okay, with dusted knives,
I will carry on..
With the mean,
In disguise.

Lone and how you remind,
Like falling stairs.
It starts with me,
And ends in jealousy.

This spirit

Gold went leaf when I decided for a golden.
A bondage with her,
At the time I thought was just with our bodies.
Later I realized some else.
So,
I cut her lips from the sky
Which was watching us
And only tearing me apart.
I put it on this doll
And sent her on a walk...
Into a search of heaven,
From where she thought she came
And she did from my eyes of love..
But no, ego never pacifies beauty.
Anyways,
The doll carried a run in this marathon...
Where my friend chaos was the judge.
He was craving disorder in new ways
As I used to feed him the same....
For years and years.
Yes, you are a good judge.
But this spirit....
Carried me on walks and some talks

And some talks more
And some talks in jealousy
And some talks more
And some talks more
Shut up.
The end?
Found it? not yet....
Some get it...eventually.
Everyone will play turns, it will come.

Queen of a butter paper

A love for me?
Like you did or said to some before
And after.
You think it's needed?
In life, to justify or accept our dependent parts.
Maybe a plan?
For example,
A queen came to the throne
And just mirrored fifty men
And a queen who came
To be herself.
Lack of faith in yourself,
Is killing you from inside.
Should I say that I can't see through?
Then you wanna be mine,
Ain't that true?
Just your eyes made me realize
It's just another learning day in our lives...
You, queen of a butter paper.

Focus on your developing hell,
You belong in the daylight.
Trouble isn't much for you.
Hesitation isn't what you know.
Beautiful friends with stern lives,
Money on steak.
I will complicate you,
Fall for me and you won't fall asleep.
I will dwell with my nature,
Maybe it does set me free.

As it was a beginning which I presumed into,
A new dawn will meow my way for some sweetheart.
But again, I'm still weak...
Can't help falling for illusions.
Back in the cycle.
Then I had some time off...
From myself and myself
But it only becomes more lethal
And you just prayed for him.
I got a plain text saying,
One second or third night...
A fourth gate to foresight.
Do I make sense?
I always do,
I always fucking do.

Cut you like cold wood

Turbulence, on shores...
Stomach with only water up till this high head.
Banner in hands with red...
Not in blood but with spirit.
A mountain to climb
And I'll cut you like cold wood.

Scared some sequences with courage.
Height of insanity or a lover in madness,
Fell into the already owned or escapism,
And lies....they just blamed.
No.

Night after night,
Day in and day out...
Axe fell in battle,
Axe didn't get the last laugh.
Nature deprived and of course of love.
Palms acupuncture to accept reality.
Heavy energy but only ever longing.
Bring it on again...
And I'll cut you like cold wood.

I cling onto

I cling onto,
To impress my mind.
I think it's not good by itself.

I worry for two,
In the name of facts.
I think of us in them.

I tear down trash,
To feel boldness.
It's not here.

I stick to nature,
For truth and peace
It's pulling me in.

Evenings went,
One after another,
It doesn't work out.

My anger eats the flesh.
Care I say...
Care, for what? Or a better word for whom?

Fixed with both sides

Imagine a world where everyone had a roof over,
And a heart to look after or look by.
To which they always have some for themselves,
When the days aren't bright for days....

Well, that's a good use of imagination there
But where will the money come from and why would
You wanna do that? he said.

I am just trying to help you see the future..
You were there for a minute,
In my emotional context.
This way is my satisfaction,
This way is to our satisfaction.

Yeah.....no, he said.
Waking up every day with practicality
And skills are good..
I don't wanna stay here anymore,
You know it too.
You can try to play it all the time but
Can't be happy with this.
Hehe.
About time before the melting point.
Fuck off. Where's the weed? he said.

Strings

A caravan rescued us from the depth.
Falling apart.
Her love flower from lake to tomorrow,
Her love craves ocean now.
I cut my skin up to make it follow patterns.
There were always better ways to go about it...
But I guess a haywire from the past,
Won't end like us forever.
Her hair was bright,
As if they planned all night...
To melt the sun..
I can see some future,
From here to there
And there to you.
Some still had us.
We won.

No one without no other

I have been asked to dry my hair up,
While I ran on bays.
To be present when nothing is shining
And be away when everything was worth living for.

I have been told to say this,
When the moment is now a past.
To say that when this comes again,
It never will, I conquered the scars.

I have been on a rest when all i dreamt was life,
To live this and not live on the other side,
All the time.

I have been realized that holding used to be becomes painful,
It doesn't happen to everybody,
So early.
Away I said take me,
When my heart was lost in my body
And head had nothing but love and nobody.

So, you see,

A cage you live in when darkness
Was holding my left hand but eyes always
Looked for the outside.
A light you live in until it becomes empty
And time says midnight.
Can't get one without the other...
No one without no other.

Hypocrisy

I waited in many minds.
In this dark blue sedan,
Smoking and playing electronics.
Just so I don't indulge in the current time,
So, it passes me by.
And then you,
For you.

There you were,
In that long dress
With the shiny hair not more than my love for you.

And just so I found out later on,
How quickly I change my extremes..
From dark and intense
To Ohhh......hmmm.
That's what you do to me,
But a hypocrite me.

Can't go on without you

I walked up till the end of March...
Some people lied and sometimes even my heart.
I never really notice days.
Living with deceit and having a deception
For my company.
I can deal with.
Put a toss to hurt or play a draw.
I can't go on without you,
Very easy to see.

Spring would be sunshine and disaster would be nights.
Why do I always end up on this slice?
Ever wondered why this keeps coming up,
With some sugar or a glass of wine and no rubber.
Life has endless days and endless for some while,
Still nothing in this small time.
I can't go on without you,
Very easy to see.

I dare not to step in the sun.
Pierces my head which was a cat with a gun.
I fell back to here again...

Pretend that I don't care but I don't.
To feel is such a pain.
Oh! How dreadful it is,
If you born this way
Or just the opposite with a touch of bliss.
People like us will never die,
Only when happiness is tomorrow for them.
I can't go on without you,
Very easy to see.

True story

God fulfills all the dreams you dream of...
The ones you keep it your heart and
Take it around every day.
And then give complimentary ones too...
Just out of love for your devotion to yourself.
So, chill.

Die young and leave a pure looking corpse

I could probably say the same thing about me.
Journey in exile or adapting to peace.
Can you say it?
I wonder if we die young, remind me.

I could probably say the same words..
Like you can find me.
Living in jars and living past, ease.
Eating in cars and guarding our sleep.
I hate staying up,
I hate staying up.

I could probably say the same thing on decrease.
Fridays on full time and hair left greased.
Sparrow starts to run and plays in green.
Cut the wings?
Wonder if we die young, remind me.

Do you really understand me?

I was not able to make a manage.
So, it ain't much of a problem.
After this,
I will run to the kitchen
And make myself ready for a voting clash.
It's hard to say what I meant by this
Or what I usually mean...
But that's like I guess an am,
As usually seen...
Hard to get,
Hard to love.
Hard to forget
And a horde of trouble.

Oii ego, what you writing?

Every time they wanna pop a smoke,
They went to the washroom.
Laughing and talking with lights in their hands,
Every couple hours.

A usual trick of throwing the cigarette in the pot
And then returning to the chambers..
Of their whatever.

I would be lost and I had to pee.
It's like I do it upon the words their lips pass...
The life they recall,
What they call life.
From the deformity till the judgment.
It feels great....
It's the good thing, today.

Far away in the wind.
These wounds will not heal.
Tired and all insane,
These wounds will not heal.
Ever and ever, I wake
Cursing the game.
These moods they feel.
Ram and ram, my head
Filling the skies.
I camouflage the sun..
Nothing's real.

Petty little me

Adored by the beauty of flowers,
Lost in the fragrance of love.
Drowns when the moon is down,
Uplifts in the opposite.
Oh! Petty little me.

Jealousy in useless deeds,
Blames karma and desires higher beliefs.
Craves for material yet disgusts you,
Always playing in virtual reality.
Oh! Petty little me.

Easy come Easy go.
Neither forgives nor forgets.
Pretends to sack and doing undo,
Revenge always living next room.
Oh! Petty little me.

Cry for the broken yet won't help himself.
Often bury light in other,
Yet always in darkness.
Inside a well
And outside a desert,
Where will you go with your petty little me?

Girl with raven colored hair

Girl would laugh out loud.
Went on and held a guy's hand,
He deals proud.
Listens to songs about despair and emptiness,
She wasn't any.
You way too positive...and multiply two.
She said she loves me
And more so of the way I sound.
A change in her personality,
When the world would leave her to me.
Would prefer colors...
Colors called this blue and white and red
But ended up falling for goth play guys like myself.
Oh! You wanna put black paint now, don't you?
Girl would like to party.
Down by the fourth block up left..
She went missing,
Just pretending to have nobody.
In a way I would like this to sound....
More in love and not judgmental.
But that's how I express dear,
You can't really be put into words.
So there,
The beauty.

A peaceful imagination

A day to remember came by, at last.
A step closer to what I thought wasn't there.
With the heaven full of blues
And mountains I thought were far, but just standing tall.
With the breeze taking my hair from left and right
And as far as I could see it was green.
A nature.
And animals were eating what they were supposed to
And not what they have to.
Looked happy.
A new culture around and some better...
Knowledgeable from the old, I know.
It's funny how they gave them the stare of
Outcasts and rejects like me.
Funny,
And will never know the passion.
And love,
I was sitting here on top of this,
With a cigarette in my left hand
Enjoying the mental peace,
Which i conquered from all my pieces,
And I am just getting started.

Phoenix

When everything went down...
Everything you were and everyone you saw
Or believed in,
Everything you dreamt of
And all of you falls apart.
When there isn't hope for anything in you
And all the doors are locked,
Just for you to sit and wonder in what's left..
And what's left is nothing.
It all has been burned and turned to ashes,
With your truth in it.
Well, my friend...
It's time for the phoenix to rise,
In whose charm you will be stunned
And awed by the beauty of feathers
Which falls down in the last of your past.

One side to another.
Twelve past eighteen,
Perfect timing.
I guess I'm not drunk enough.
Coral fishes eaten by suicidal obesity.
Another pleasure of life,
For being a witness to this scene.
Zodiac checks to see if i should develop...
Trust.
I don't wanna fall in the morning,
With a little sense of what was happening.
Oh! Another glass of whiskey....
Thank you very much.
Maybe, I did choose this life.

Angry, get over it

Slut plays this then slut plays that,
Woolen socks but an empty thrash.
Guys would cage,
Guys rose to date trees and daydreams,
Grandma never went past the fourth week.
Now you wonder what I mean?
Bet your head is a nut...
Now I'll play the part..
Told your life and how much it is in a jar.
Do you believe it?
Am I faking it?
Faking for what?
I can get what I want, when I want it..
You know this...
You wanna know this.

Oh! In the middle of a running thought,
You judge.
You judging?
My sweet self-appointed staff.
Mockery of you made on the streets and with style.
You can't drive cars over floods,
Accept the fine.

Herself a divine.
I will sell my body to you, right?
Take my mother,
Bet you wanna take my time.
Snow went five centimeters up...
These feet aren't getting clustered,
They climb over your head when I'm drowning.

You don't know

Many minds,
Many trees would also pass me by.
Hoping and imagining the rhythm.
Many minds,
For days and days to droughts and years..
Into the deep waters
And flooding transylvania.
Never I thought the end,
Never did I care for it...
A wall I built around,
And everything you do is kept inside and safe.
You won't know what a mother would do.
You were lost in admiration and bargain exchange,
On images.
Now you think and made me one too.
Letting go scares me.
Letting go is an art I need to possess.
Bitterness and jealousy is what's left.
Not a big deal
But remember I'll still accept you,
Bye.

Just eight and eight stuff

I put up a friendship with strangeness.
He loves me though I hate myself.
I would often lie and believe in the morning
But he took my heart way far off,
I can't even imagine.
Often, he acts as a smoother of charm,
Made me believe I am damned
Without her arms.
Then flipped a coin he said he took from the stars.
I would seldom lose but I don't care,
As an outcast.
But of course with money,
Walked in the green with warmness.
Snakes covered themselves on my legs.
I wanna see the best you can do now,
Desires are just a deception.

Cut the chase, back to my place

Hey, check out this matter of day.
Looks like another girl, a banger, may?
Wanna hold my wrist, no?
A little fable shit and a playdate strip.
Witty, canned and solitude
But the way she climbs up and down
These rooms.
Looking like one of those pretty get go's...
Steps on the slips on a male day,
Greeks had an army and married days.
Man, like I know,
Cut to chase back to my place.
I wore my paddless jealousy
And plus, I got a pal in this gals game.
In fact, he is the one writing this for you.
Bye, girl.

Into a rage, I fly

Into a rage, I fly.
My baby never understood how come?
My baby's first time with an ocean.
But servants said the obvious...
Lovely face
And outgoing dear.
The president did well,
Outcome was written without the open mind
And truth,
Covered with insecurities.
You won't really smother me.
Like to but it wouldn't do,
Take turns by playing fools.
Don't regret a trip
And I got this friend, you see
Who makes me feel...
Then I wanted more than I would steal.
To arrest myself in the morning routine
And going out of my way
To prove you I still,
Care about you.

Never,

Tell me what I wanna hear.
Ask much then run from the thrill
Wish I could do, but I don't.
Don't regret a thing
And my friend you see,
Who makes me feel...
And then I arranged meetings with the evening fears.
I'll go out of my way,
To prove you I still,
Care about you.

Author's bio:

I was born in New Delhi.

It's my second poetry book.